HUNTING DOGS

TERRIERS
LOYAL HUNTING COMPANIONS

BY GAIL LANGER KARWOSKI

CAPSTONE PRESS
a capstone imprint

Edge Books are published by Capstone Press,
1710 Roe Crest Drive, North Mankato, Minnesota 56003
www.capstonepub.com

Library of Congress Cataloging-in-Publication Data
CIP information on file with the Library of Congress
ISBN 978-1-4296-9989-1 (library binding)
ISBN 978-1-62065-939-7 (paper over board)
ISBN 978-1-4765-1551-9 (eBook PDF)

Editorial Credits
Angie Kaelberer, editor; Kyle Grenz, designer; Marcie Spence, media researcher;
Jennifer Walker, production specialist

Photo Credits
Christine Hayden, 14, 21, 22, 23; Dreamstime: Piter77, 15; iStockphoto: TheBiggles,
5; Shutterstock: AnetaPics, 10 (right), Claudia Steininger, 12, cynoclub, 27, 28, djem,
18, eAlisa, front cover, Four Oaks, 1, godrick, back cover, Jack Scrivener, 6-7, JD,
11 (middle), Laura Maeva, 13 (right), Lee O'Dell, 8-9, lightpoet, 13 (left), Markku
Vitikainen, 11 (top), Nagy Melinda, 24, ncn18, 11 (bottom), Olga_i, 29, Perig, 25,
PHB.cz (Richard Semik), 16 (top), photocell, 10 (left), Reddogs, 16 (bottom), Sandra
zuerlein, 20, Serdar Tibet, 26, Sergey Sukhorukov, 19, Sue Robinson, 4

Capstone Press thanks Bruce Tolhurst of the American Hunting Dog Club for his
assistance with this book.

Printed in the United States of America in Stevens Point, Wisconsin.
092012   006937WZS13

The hunter listened to the radio beeps that signaled her dog's location underground. When the terrier stopped moving, the hunter began to dig. Both the hunter and the terrier knew what to do. The terrier's job was to locate the fox, and the hunter's job was to remove it.

gone to ground—when a terrier follows a wild animal underground

5

TERRIER HISTORY

Terriers were bred to hunt vermin. These nuisance mammals are a threat to a farmer's livestock or crops. Many vermin, such as foxes and badgers, live in underground burrows. To hunt them, terriers must be small enough to push through a narrow tunnel and fierce enough to face a vicious opponent. No wonder some people call the terrier "a big dog in a small dog's body!"

Lakeland terrier

6

People developed the first terriers in the 1500s. Over time breeders created the hunting terrier by selecting the smaller and braver dogs in each litter. Most terriers were developed in the United Kingdom, but a few breeds came from Germany, Australia, Czechoslovakia, and other countries.

Tale of a Terrier

In 1777 American soldiers found a terrier wandering on a Pennsylvania battlefield during the Revolutionary War (1775–1783) battle of Germantown. The dog's collar showed that it belonged to British General William Howe.

The soldiers brought the dog to their commander, General George Washington. The general had the dog fed and brushed. Then he ordered a cease-fire and returned the terrier to Howe, along with a personal note.

7

DEN TRIALS

The American Kennel Club (AKC) recognizes 28 breeds in the terrier group. Today some people still use their terriers to hunt vermin. But most terriers in the United States are family pets or show dogs rather than hunting dogs. Non-hunting terriers can still show their hunting skills at den trial competitions. Young terriers start out by running through wooden tunnels about 10 feet (3 meters) long. As their skills progress, the dogs search for caged rats in longer tunnels with more twists and turns.

The American Working Terrier Association (AWTA) was founded to preserve and encourage hunting terriers. Its den trials are open to 20 terrier breeds, as well as smaller mixed-breed terriers and dachshunds. The dogs earn titles for finding game and holding it at bay, which means they corner the game and keep it at a safe distance away.

The Jack Russell Terrier Club of America (JRTCA) tests the hunting abilities of Russell terriers. JRTCA competitions include racing and agility events as well as den trials.

TERRIER BREEDS

Breed	Country of Origin	Life Expectancy
Airedale	England	13 years
American Staffordshire	United States	12 years
Australian	Australia	14 years
Bedlington	England	14–15 years
Border	England	13–14 years
Bull (and miniature bull)	England	11-13 years
Cairn	Scotland	14 years
Cesky	Czech Republic	12-14 years
Dandie Dinmont	Scotland	14 years
Fell *	England	11-13 years
Fox (both smooth and wirehaired)	England	13-14 years
Glen of Imaal	Ireland	13-14 years
Irish	Ireland	13 years

Wirehaired fox

Smooth fox

Breed	Country of Origin	Life Expectancy
Jagd *	Germany	14 years
Kerry Blue	Ireland	14 years
Lakeland	England	13-14 years
Manchester	England	13-14 years
Miniature Schnauzer	Germany	14 years
Norfolk	England	14 years
Norwich	England	14 years
Russell (both Jack and Parson)	England	13-14 years
Patterdale	England	11-13 years
Scottish	Scotland	13-14 years
Sealyham	Wales	15 years
Skye	Scotland	13 years
Soft-coated Wheaten	Ireland	12-15 years
Staffordshire Bull	England	12-14 years
Welsh	Wales	10-12 years
West Highland White	Scotland	14 years

*recognized only by the AWTA

Jack Russell

Patterdale

West Highland white

11

CHAPTER 2

THE DOWN-TO-EARTH DOG

Terriers were developed for hunting different types of **quarry**. Larger breeds are used to hunt above ground. Their quarry includes rats, squirrels, rabbits, and birds. Airedales are the largest terriers. This breed was developed in Great Britain to hunt otters.

Male Airedales are about 23 inches (58 centimeters) tall.

EARTHDOGS

Many terrier breeds were developed for hunting quarry in underground dens. These "earthdogs" include the border, cairn, and Jack Russell.

DOG FACT

Jack Russell and Parson Russell terriers were named for avid foxhunter Parson John Russell. Russell lived in England during the 1800s.

Earthdogs must be small enough to move through a cramped tunnel. Underground, size can mean the difference between life and death. A terrier that is too

large could get stuck and suffocate. But if the terrier is too small, it may not be able to defend itself against a dangerous opponent such as a fox or badger.

Border terriers are known for their easygoing personalities.

To compete in a den trial, a terrier needs to be able to get through a tunnel measuring 9 inches (23 cm) high and wide. Most earthdogs stand about 12 inches (30 cm) tall. But a dog's chest size is more important, because the chest is the thickest part of a dog's body. An earthdog's chest **circumference** should be no more than 14 inches (36 cm).

Cairns were bred to dig in rocky soil.

quarry—a wild animal that is hunted

circumference—the measurement around something

13

FINDING AND TRACKING

A hunting terrier mainly uses its nose to find quarry. By sniffing a burrow's entrance, a terrier can tell whether its quarry is inside.

Earthdogs bark to communicate with their handlers and to keep quarry at bay. A dog wears a radio transmitter on its collar for safety. But the dog's bark is important in case this equipment fails. Sometimes a dog is unwilling or unable to bark. The handler then could lose track of the dog.

Collar radio transmitters help protect earthdogs.

ABILITIES

The **temperament** of a hunting terrier is very important. When a terrier faces quarry underground, it acts alone. For this reason, earthdogs were bred to be independent. But a hunting dog must also obey commands. A terrier that chases a farmer's pet cat won't be a success in the field!

temperament—the combination of a dog's behavior and personality

14

Earthdogs need to be adaptable. Earthdogs work in darkness, in unfamiliar surroundings, and in the quarry's home ground. No two tunnels will be the same shape or length. The quarry might hole up in a corner or turn and attack. The quarry may be bigger than the dog. The terrier's job is to remain with the quarry, even if it bites or claws, until its owner can dig down to it.

Hunting is an instinct that a dog is born with. In some terriers, the instinct is so strong that they try to kill the animals they hunt. But a farmer may want the vermin removed rather than destroyed. A "hard" terrier—one that wants to fight with the quarry—won't get the job done.

Like all hunting dogs, terriers need energy and endurance. A hunt may last many hours over rough ground and in bad weather.

CHOOSING A HUNTING TERRIER

The best way to find a hunting terrier is from a breeder with a good reputation. You can find the names of terrier breeders through hunting dog organizations. Always visit the breeder's kennel, and if possible, meet the puppy's parents. If the parents are skilled hunting dogs, their pups will likely be good hunters as well.

Choose a puppy that is alert, friendly, and playful. It should not be afraid of noises or new people and situations. Drop an object such as a cooking pot several feet away from the pups. If a puppy immediately runs to investigate the noise, it will likely make a good hunter.

EARTHDOG TITLES

Award	Organization	Quarry	Requirements
Junior Earthdog	American Kennel Club (AKC)	caged rat	Dog crawls through simple tunnel within 30 seconds and stays with quarry for 60 seconds.
Senior Earthdog	AKC	caged rat	Dog crawls through complex tunnel within 15 seconds and stays with quarry for 90 seconds.
Master Earthdog	AKC	caged rat	Two dogs take turns crawling through obstructed tunnels within 90 seconds and staying with quarry for 90 seconds.
Trial Certificate	Jack Russell Terrier Club of America (JRTCA)	caged rat	Dog earns a 100 percent score in the open class of a Go-to-Ground den trial.
Sporting Certificate	JRTCA	squirrels, rats	Dog tracks quarry either above ground or in a wooden tunnel.
Natural Hunting Certificate Below Ground in the Field	JRTCA	foxes, badgers, raccoons, woodchucks	Dog keeps quarry at bay in natural den.
Bronze Working Terrier Medallion for Special Merit in the Field	JRTCA	foxes, badgers, raccoons, woodchucks	Three natural hunting certificates for different quarry.
Working Certificate	American Working Terrier Association (AWTA)	foxes, badgers, raccoons, woodchucks	Dog keeps quarry at bay in natural den.
Hunting Certificate	AWTA	above-ground quarry such as groundhogs, rabbits, and squirrels	Dog participates in at least six hunts during a hunting season.
Veteran Earthdog Award	AWTA	three different quarry animals	Dog with 10 working certificates.

CHAPTER 3

TRAINING A HUNTING TERRIER

The most important part of training is to have a good relationship with your dog. But that doesn't mean you should allow your dog to do whatever it wants. Like their wolf ancestors, dogs are pack animals. Each pack has a leader. In your dog's eyes, that leader should be you.

Begin each training with a short walk or play time. Exercise will help your puppy get rid of energy so it can focus. Puppies learn best in short, frequent sessions. Spend no more than 15 minutes training at a time.

BASIC TRAINING

Before learning to hunt, your terrier needs to know basic obedience commands such as come, sit, stay, and lie down. Your dog also needs to learn to **heel**.

Before giving a command, get your puppy's attention by calling its name. Maintaining eye contact with your terrier will help keep its attention on you. Always say the command with the same wording and tone of voice. As soon as your puppy performs the desired action, reward it with praise and

a small food treat. Terriers are fast learners but also can become bored easily. Rewards will help your dog stay on track.

Some advanced obedience lessons are also important. A hunting terrier needs to stay close to its owner when walking off leash. It shouldn't chase pets or livestock. It also shouldn't scare off quarry by barking when above ground.

heel—a command telling a dog to walk by a person's side

HUNTER TRAINING

Most terriers begin to show an interest in hunting when they are about a year old. One way a puppy shows hunting interest is by sniffing the ground in search of quarry.

You can encourage your puppy to follow quarry by dragging a fur piece along the ground. To teach a dog to find quarry by smell, some trainers use scented spray purchased at a hunting store. Spray a furry toy with the scent of the quarry that the terrier will hunt. After letting the dog sniff the toy, hide it behind a fence or tree. When your terrier finds the toy, reward it with praise and a treat.

Trainers often use live rats from pet stores to teach a dog to **mark** quarry. Put the rat in a secure cage. After the puppy shows interest by approaching and sniffing, hold the puppy back until it barks and paws at the cage.

Never let your puppy bite or kill the rat used in training. An earthdog's job is to find and keep the quarry at bay, not kill it. And if a rat bites your pup, the dog may develop a lifelong fear.

mark—to bark and paw when quarry is located

EARTHDOG TRAINING

If your terrier will hunt underground, you can build a tunnel called a liner to use in training. A liner can be made of a plastic pipe with a wide opening, planks of wood nailed together, or cardboard boxes taped together to form a tunnel with open ends. Some people bury liners made of pipe or wood under a few inches of soil to resemble the conditions in an actual hunt.

Allow your terrier to train at its own pace.

Encourage your puppy to go inside the liner by dragging a toy on a string or placing a food treat inside. Just have your terrier go a couple of feet into the tunnel at first. As it gets more comfortable, put the treat or toy deeper inside the tunnel. When your pup makes it all the way through the tunnel, praise it and give it a **jackpot** of treats. If your puppy hesitates, try starting with a wider tunnel or wait a few days and try again.

Once your puppy is comfortable running through the liner, make the game more interesting. Attach another box to the liner to form a right-angle turn. Add animal scent with a spray bought at a hunting store. You can also put a rat or a squirrel in a secure cage at the end of the tunnel. Make sure the cage or box is sturdy enough to keep your dog from biting or hurting the animal inside.

Many trainers think it's helpful to have a puppy watch an experienced terrier at work either at an event or in the field. You can find events and hunters through hunting terrier associations.

Building a Training Tunnel

With an adult's help, you can build a liner to train your terrier to hunt underground. A sturdy tunnel can be built from 5/8-inch (1.6-cm) plywood and drywall screws. A tunnel that is 6 feet (1.8 meters) long and 9 inches (23 cm) tall and wide is the perfect size for training most terriers.

jackpot—a large number of something

CHAPTER 4

YOUR TERRIER AT HOME

All dogs need regular care at home and checkups by a veterinarian. The vet will vaccinate your terrier against rabies and other diseases. Since hunting terriers come into contact with wild animals, it's especially important for your dog to be up to date on vaccinations. Give your terrier preventive medications each month to protect it from fleas, ticks, and heartworms.

All dog breeds can have health problems. Large terriers like Airedales can develop **hip dysplasia**. Smaller terriers may develop **patellar luxation**. Ask your breeder if your puppy's parents have been tested and cleared for these conditions.

FEEDING

Feed your terrier high-quality food. Some terrier breeds have allergies that affect their skin or digestion. Dog food made without allergy-causing ingredients such as grain can help clear up these problems.

Some terrier breeds, such as the cairn, tend to put on weight. Overweight dogs have more health problems and also can get stuck in holes while hunting.

Your dog's appearance is the best way to judge if it is at a healthy weight. Its ribs shouldn't stick out, but you should be able to feel them under a layer of muscle.

hip dysplasia—a condition in which an animal's hip joints do not fit together properly

patellar luxation—a dislocated kneecap

GROOMING

Begin short grooming sessions as soon as you get your terrier puppy. Reward your puppy for being calm when brushed.

Some terrier breeds, such as Patterdales, have short, smooth coats. Others, such as cairn terriers, have longer, rough coats. Some terriers, including the fox and Jack Russell, are bred to have either smooth or rough coats.

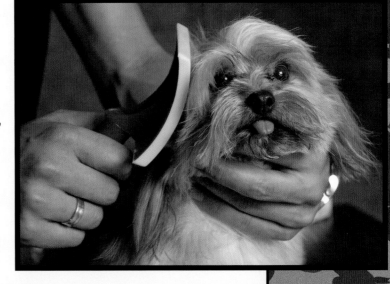

During shedding season, some of your terrier's hairs will die and fall out. Grooming a rough-coated terrier involves **stripping**. It can be done either by hand or with a stripping tool. Strip a terrier's coat every two to three months.

strip—to pluck dead hair from a dog's coat

After a hunt or walk, check your terrier for ticks. Ticks can latch on anywhere, but they often are found on a dog's ears, neck, chest, and toes. Gently remove ticks with tweezers.

A smooth-coated Jack Russell's fur usually doesn't need to be stripped.

Your terrier should need a bath only every few months, unless it gets into something very dirty or smelly. After a hunt, your terrier's skin may be scratched from branches and brush. A medicated shampoo will help prevent the scratches from becoming infected.

EXERCISE

A hunting terrier needs regular exercise. You won't hunt or train every day, but you can keep your terrier fit with daily walks and playtime. Keep games lively and interesting so your terrier won't get bored. Many terriers also do well at agility competitions.

Manchester terrier at an agility event

Hunting with your terrier can be fun for both of you. A day in the field or at a den trial allows your terrier to explore its hunting instincts. You'll get exercise and maybe make some new friends. Best of all, you'll enjoy quality time with your dog.

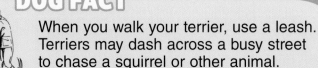

DOG FACT

When you walk your terrier, use a leash. Terriers may dash across a busy street to chase a squirrel or other animal.

FIRST AID WHILE HUNTING

Injury	Symptoms	First Aid
foot injury	lameness	Flush paw with warm water; apply antibacterial ointment and bandage
insect sting	swelling, redness	Remove stinger by brushing with stiff paper or credit card. Apply a paste of baking soda and water for bee sting or vinegar for wasp sting. If head or neck swells, get the dog to a vet quickly.
snakebite	swelling, fang marks, nausea, weakness	Try to identify the snake. Keep the dog quiet and get it to a vet quickly.
wound	bleeding	Cover wound with a clean cloth and apply pressure. If bleeding continues or the cut is deep, get dog to vet quickly.
heatstroke	breathing rapidly and loudly, thick saliva, bright red gums, vomiting	Place a cool, wet towel around the dog's neck and head. When the dog is cooler, immerse it in cool (not icy) water. Get it to a vet as quickly as possible.
hypothermia	paleness, shivering, sluggish movements	Wrap the dog in a heated blanket and give it warm fluids to drink.

GLOSSARY

agility (uh-GI-luh-tee)—competitions in which dogs race through a series of obstacles

circumference (sur-KUHM-fur-uhnss)—the measurement around something

gone to ground (GAWN TO GROUND)–when a terrier follows a wild animal underground

heel (HEEL)—a command telling a dog to walk by a person's side

hip dysplasia (HIP dis-PLAY-zhah)—a condition in which an animal's hip joints do not fit together properly

jackpot (JAK-pot)—a large number of something

mark (MAHRK)—to bark and paw when quarry is located

patellar luxation (puh-TEH-lahr luk-SAY-shuhn)—a dislocated kneecap

quarry (KWOR-ee)—a wild animal that is hunted

strip (STRIP)—to pluck dead hair from a dog's coat

temperament (tem-PUHR-uh-muhnt)—the combination of a dog's behavior and personality

vermin (VUR-min)—a wild mammal that threatens a farmer's livestock or crops

READ MORE

Frier-Murza, Jo Ann. *Earthdog Ins and Outs.* Crosswicks, N.J.: VGF Publications, 2010.

Gagne, Tammy. *Jack Russell Terriers.* All about Dogs. Mankato, Minn.: Capstone Press, 2009.

Green, Sara. *West Highland White Terriers.* Blastoff! Readers: Dog Breeds. Minneapolis: Bellwether Media, 2010.

INTERNET SITES

FactHound offers a safe, fun way to find Internet sites related to this book. All of the sites on FactHound have been researched by our staff.

Here's all you do:

Visit *www.facthound.com*

Type in this code: 9781429699891

 **Super-cool stuff!** Check out projects, games and lots more at **www.capstonekids.com**

INDEX